Faithfully Affirmed

Copyright © 2024 by Skyy Danielle

All rights reserved. Aside from brief passages in a published review, no part of this book may be reproduced or transmitted in any form or by any means - electronic, mechanical, photocopy, recording, scanning or any other technologies known or later developed, without written permission from the author, Skyy Danielle.

Ignited Ink 717 LLC
Houston, TX

Cover Design: Ebony Rose of Ignited Ink 717 LLC
Cover Photography: Different Mind Designs

Categories:

Skyy is available for keynotes, panels, book talks, and workshops.

Discounts for bulk purchases of 25 books or more are available.
Visit IgnitedInk717.com to learn more and place an order.

For reprint permission, write to IgnitedInk717@gmail.com
Library of Congress Control Number: Proof

ISBN, print: Proof
ISBN, ebook: Proof

Printed in the United States of America

DEDICATION

For the me who needs to be poured into.

For the you who knows how it feels to need community to help you push through.

May this bring us a new sense a power, peace and balance.

FOREWORD

Whooodaaawhoooo! In the tapestry of existence, we are threads woven together by the cosmic forces that bind us—forces that flow through us, animating our spirits and shaping our destinies. Yet, amidst the ebb and flow of life's currents, we often find ourselves adrift, buffeted by the storms of pain and turmoil that assail our souls. It is in these moments of darkness that we yearn for a guiding light, a beacon of hope to lead us back to ourselves.

Skyy designed the pages of *Faithfully Affirmed* to be such a beacon—a map to navigate the labyrinth of our inner world, to traverse the pathways of healing and self-discovery. Drawing upon the ancient wisdom of the chakras and the transformative power of affirmations, she offers a roadmap for those seeking to reclaim their wholeness and embrace the fullness of their being.

At the heart of this journey lies the understanding that we are not merely physical beings, but energetic beings intricately connected to the vast web of existence. The chakras, spinning wheels of energy that reside within us, serve as gateways to our deepest truths, each one holding the key to unlocking a different aspect of our consciousness. By tending to these energy centers with care and intention, we open ourselves to the flow of universal energy, allowing it to cleanse, heal, and rejuvenate us from within.

But healing is not merely a matter of addressing physical ailments; it is a holistic process that encompasses the body, mind, and spirit. And so, in conjunction with the balancing of our chakras, we harness the power of affirmations—words imbued with the potent energy of intention—to reprogram the patterns of thought and belief that have kept us bound in suffering. Through the repetition of these affirmations, we plant the seeds of healing in the fertile soil of our subconscious, nurturing them with love and compassion until they blossom into manifestations of our highest potential.

The Faithfully Affirmed journal reminded me that healing is a journey, not a destination. It is a process of discovery and growth, and one that requires patience, compassion, and self-love. As you work with your chakras and say your affirmations I hope that you will find a deeper sense of connection to yourself and the world around you, and that you will continue to cultivate a practice of self-care and self-love that will serve you for the rest of your life.

The *Faithfully Affirmed* journal is an invitation to embark on a journey of self-discovery and spiritual growth. By exploring the depths of the chakras through poetry and affirmations, you will gain a deeper understanding of the intricate web of energies that shape our lives. May the wisdom of the chakras guide us towards a more profound connection with ourselves, each other, and the universe.

PREFACE

This book was necessary for all the times I wanted to give up and tried to give up because I felt alone. For all the times I didn't recognize the reflection in the mirror. For all the times I reached my hands out hoping someone would hold them and remind me of the power within me. It was no fun feeling like all the healing I done was for nothing. For quite some time it seemed that the healthy coping skills I developed were null and void. My balance was *gone*. My peace was *gone*. My confidence was *gone*. My voice was *gone*. I was *gone*. And it seemed like no matter what I tried I was broken down more and more.

One day I was thinking about how I would listen to affirmations and healing frequencies daily to help me stay and/or get balanced. Also to manifest. I figured if I could find a video or podcast with "*YOU ARE*" affirmations it would help me a ton since my hands still seem to be floating in the air. As I searched for this I had no luck. I then heard God tell me that it is a part of my purpose to help fill this void and chakras would be the focus for this project. Look, I had done research on chakras before so I was no stranger to them but really God. Me? Needless to say, I was obedient.

Disclaimer: I was not then and still am not a chakra guru. I will forever be a student learning what I can in life. So as you utilize this daily affirmation book know that we are on this journey together. If you want to continue on this journey be sure to tap into the Faithfully Affirmed podcast on all major platforms.

Enjoy!

CONNECT

ROOT CHAKRA

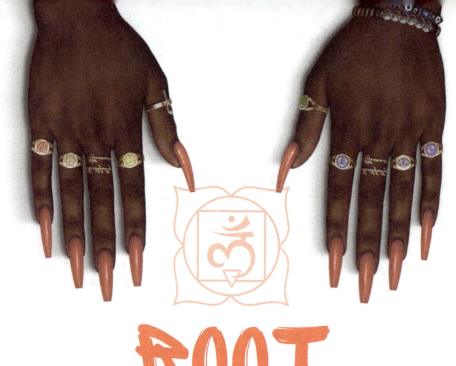

ROOT

TO BE GROUNDED IN SELF
I MASSAGE
THE BASE OF MY SPINE
THIS TELLS ME THAT I AM SAFE
AND CAN SURRENDER TO THE DIVINE

MORE CHAKRA INFORMATION AND REFLECTION PAGES AVAILABLE IN YOUR FAITHFULLY AFFIRMED JOURNAL

ROOT

YOU ARE SAFE

ROOT

DAY 2

YOUR BODY ALWAYS TAKES CARE OF YOU BECAUSE YOU TAKE CARE OF IT

ROOT

YOU GROUND YOURSELF WITH POSITIVITY AND EXHALE THE NEGATIVITY

ROOT

DAY 4

YOU ARE PROTECTED

ROOT

DAY 5

YOU ARE SUPPORTED BY THE EARTH

ROOT

YOU ARE COMMITTED TO FULFILLING YOUR LIFE'S PURPOSE

ROOT

DAY 7

HOW DO YOU UNINTENTIONALLY ALLOW OTHERS TO INVADE YOUR PERSONAL BOUNDARIES?

ROOT

DAY 8

YOU ARE CONNECTED AND GUIDED BY MOTHER EARTH

ROOT

YOU TRUST YOURSELF

ROOT

DAY 10

NO MATTER WHERE YOU GO YOU ARE AT HOME IN YOURSELF

ROOT

DAY 11

NO MATTER WHAT STORMS MAY COME, YOU ARE ROOTED IN THE EARTH AND YOU ARE SAFE

ROOT

DAY 12

YOU ARE EQUIPPED WITH ALL THE TOOLS YOU NEED TO SUCCEED

ROOT

ALL YOUR NEEDS ARE MET

ROOT

DAY 14

HOW DO YOU COMMUNICATE YOUR BOUNDARIES TO OTHERS?

ROOT

YOU ARE EXACTLY WHERE YOU ARE MEANT TO BE

ROOT

DAY 16

YOUR BODY IS A SAFE AND WORTHY HOME FOR YOUR SPIRIT

ROOT

YOU ARE WHOLE AND COMPLETE EXACTLY AS YOU ARE

ROOT

DAY 18

YOU HAVE ACCESS TO ALL OF THE RESOURCES THAT YOU NEED TO THRIVE

ROOT

DAY 19

YOU STILL REMAIN ROOTED TO THE EARTH EVEN WHEN THE WORLD AROUND YOU FEELS CHAOTIC

ROOT

YOU ARE GRATEFUL FOR YOUR ABILITY TO REMAIN PEACEFUL AND CALM IN ALL SITUATIONS

ROOT

DAY 21

WHAT PRACTICES IN YOUR DAILY ROUTINE CAN YOU INCORPORATE THAT PROMOTE MINDFULNESS AND HELP YOU REMAIN IN THE PRESENT MOMENT?

ROOT

DAY 22

YOU HAVE A DEEP CONNECTION TO MOTHER EARTH

ROOT

FINANCIAL SECURITY BELONGS TO YOU

ROOT

DAY 24

YOU ARE A SPIRITUAL BEING THAT VALUES THEIR PHYSICAL BODY

ROOT

YOU ARE NOURISHED AND SUPPORTED BY MOTHER EARTH

ROOT

DAY 26

YOU LISTEN TO YOURSELF AND HONOR ALL OF YOUR NEEDS

ROOT

DAY 27

YOU LOVINGLY NOURISH AND CARE FOR YOURSELF

ROOT

DAY 28

WHAT MAKES YOU FEEL SAFE IN YOUR EXTERNAL WORLD?

WHAT ABOUT IN YOUR INTERNAL WORLD?

ROOT

DAY 29

YOU ARE COURAGEOUS

ROOT

YOU TRUST MORE AND FEAR LESS

ROOT

YOU ARE ACTUALLY DOING A GREAT JOB

ROOT

DAY 32

YOU ARE A BEING OF DIVINE LIGHT

ROOT

YOU ARE OPEN TO NEW IDEAS

ROOT

DAY 34

YOU ACCEPT GOOD HEALTH AS YOUR NATURAL STATE OF BEING

ROOT

WHAT DOES YOUR BOUNDARY LOOK LIKE AND HOW DO YOU KNOW WHEN IT IS BEING INVADED?

ROOT

YOU ARE READY TO ACCEPT DIVINE SUPPORT

ROOT

YOU ARE FINANCIALLY SECURE

ROOT

YOU ARE A POSITIVE PERSON

ROOT

DAY 39

YOU DESERVE SUCCESS

ROOT

DAY 40

YOU ARE DIVINELY GUIDED. THERE IS NO NEED TO RUSH

ROOT

YOU CAN RELAX KNOWING THAT EVERYTHING COMES TO YOU AT THE PERFECT TIME

ROOT

IN WHAT AREAS OF LIFE ARE YOU UNGROUNDED?

ROOT

SECURITY AND STABILITY FLOW INTO YOUR LIFE NOW WHICH ALLOWS YOU TO LIVE CONFIDENTLY AND CONNECTED TO WHO YOU ARE

ROOT

YOU ARE ROOTED IN THE PRESENT MOMENT

ROOT

DAY 45

YOUR BODY IS YOUR HOME. PLEDGE TO ALWAYS BUILD IT UP AND NEVER TEAR IT DOWN

ROOT

DAY 46

EVERY CELL IN YOUR BODY SUPPORTS YOUR TOTAL WELL BEING

ROOT

DAY 47

THE UNIVERSE WANTS TO SEE YOU HAPPY AND SUCCEEDING IN LIFE

ROOT

YOU FEEL AT HOME WITHIN THE WORLD AND WITHIN YOURSELF

ROOT

WHAT MAKES YOU FEEL FIRMLY GROUNDED IN SELF?

ROOT

DAY 50

YOU ARE FULL OF ENERGY, VITALITY, AND STRENGTH

ROOT

DAY 51

YOU HAVE ALL OF THE NECESSARY ENERGY TO FULFILL YOUR DREAMS

ROOT

DAY 52

YOUR FOUNDATION IS STRONG, STABLE AND POWERFUL

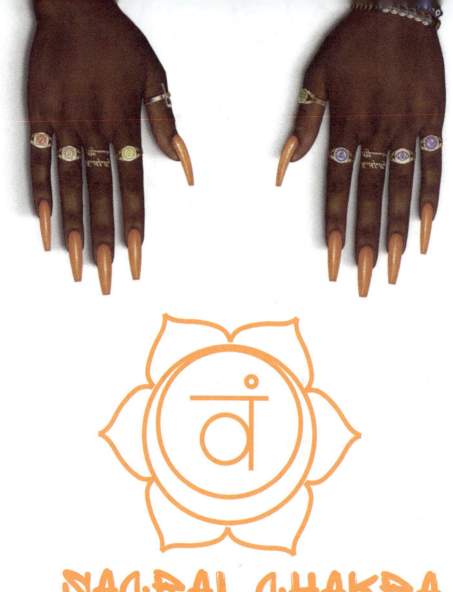

SACRAL CHAKRA

SACRAL

REACHING BEYOND THE HORIZON OF POSSIBILITIES
OPENS THE WINDOW OF JOY TO EXPOUND MY CREATIVITY
UNTIL IT RINGS FREEDOM IN 50 SHADES OF LIBERTY
FILLING ME UNTIL I FEEL EVERYTHING PASSIONATELY

MORE CHAKRA INFORMATION AND REFLECTION PAGES AVAILABLE IN YOUR FAITHFULLY AFFIRMED JOURNAL

SACRAL

YOU ARE A SACRED BEING.

SACRAL

DAY 54

YOU GIVE YOURSELF PERMISSION TO FULLY ENJOY EVERYTHING THAT YOU DO

SACRAL

YOU HONOR THE SACRED BODY IN WHICH YOUR SOUL RESIDES

SACRAL

DAY 56

WHAT AREAS OF YOUR LIFE NEED MORE PASSION?

SACRAL

YOU ALLOW CREATIVITY TO FLOW THROUGH YOU FREELY

SACRAL

DAY 58

YOU FLOW WITH GRACE AND EASE

SACRAL

DAY 59

YOU ARE OVERFLOWING WITH AN ABUNDANCE OF CREATIVE ENERGY

SACRAL

DAY 60

YOU REALIZE YOUR BODY IS A SACRED VESSEL AND YOU RESPECT IT

SACRAL

YOU ARE TUNED INTO YOUR SENSUALITY

SACRAL

YOU FEEL PLEASURE IN YOUR BODY

SACRAL

HOW CAN YOU ACTIVELY EXPRESS YOUR CREATIVITY?

SACRAL

HEALING ENERGY FLOWS THROUGH YOUR WOMB

SACRAL

YOU FALL IN LOVE WITH YOUR BEAUTY

SACRAL

DAY 66

YOU TRUST THAT YOUR LIFE IS UNFOLDING IN WONDERFUL AND JOYOUS WAYS

SACRAL

DAY 67

YOU LOVE YOUR BODY

SACRAL

DAY 68

PLEASURE IS A SACRED PART OF YOUR LIFE

SACRAL

YOU ENJOY PLEASURE IN ALL AREAS OF YOUR LIFE

SACRAL

DAY 70

HOW CAN YOU ADD MORE OPPORTUNITIES FOR PLAY IN YOUR DAILY LIFE?

SACRAL

YOU CONSISTENTLY EXUDE MORE BEAUTY AND GRACE

SACRAL

YOU ARE GRATEFUL FOR THE JOY OF BEING YOU

SACRAL

YOU HONOR YOUR DESIRES IN A NURTURING WAY

SACRAL

DAY 74

YOU ARE GRATEFUL THAT CREATIVITY NATURALLY FLOWS THROUGH YOU

SACRAL

DAY 75

YOU CONNECT WITH OTHERS WITH EASE

SACRAL

YOU SHARE LOVE WITH OTHERS AND EMBRACE INTIMACY

SACRAL

HOW DO YOU PRACTICE FORGIVENESS FOR SELF AND OTHERS?

SACRAL

YOU ARE OVERFLOWING WITH AN ABUNDANCE OF ENERGY

SACRAL

LIKE WATER YOU ARE POWERFUL YET FLUID AND FLEXIBLE

SACRAL

DAY 80

YOU LOVE TO ADMIRE FAVORITE PLACES AND PARTS OF YOUR BODY

SACRAL

DAY 81

YOU ENJOY YOUR SEXUALITY

SACRAL

DAY 82

YOU RECEIVE PLEASURE AND ABUNDANCE WITH EVERY BREATH YOU TAKE

SACRAL

DAY 83

YOU FIND JOY IN CREATING WHO YOU ARE

SACRAL

IN WHAT WAYS DOES PROSPERITY SHOW UP IN YOUR LIFE?

SACRAL

YOU ALLOW YOURSELF TO ENJOY THE SWEETNESS OF LIFE

SACRAL

YOU FALL IN LOVE WITH YOUR BEAUTY

SACRAL

YOU CHOOSE TO ENJOY WATCHING YOUR LIFE UNFOLD

SACRAL

YOU HAVE INCREDIBLE ATTRACTING POWER

SACRAL

DAY 89

YOU ENJOY THE SENSUAL PLEASURES OF LIFE

SACRAL

YOU RELEASE STUCK EMOTIONS

SACRAL

DAY 91

DO YOU BELIEVE YOU DESERVE PLEASURE IN YOUR LIFE? WHY OR WHY NOT?

(YOU DO BY THE WAY)

SACRAL

DAY 92

IN RELATIONSHIPS YOU HONOR YOUR OWN CENTER

SACRAL

DAY 93

YOUR HEALING PROCEEDS WITH GRACE

SACRAL

DAY 94

YOU ARE IN FLOW WITH THE UNIVERSE

SACRAL

YOU ARE FULLY EMBODIED

SACRAL

DAY 96

YOU POSSESS THE ABILITY, POWER AND KNOWLEDGE TO CREATE

SACRAL

YOU EMBRACE YOUR EMOTIONS WITH GRACE AND LOVE

SACRAL

HOW IS YOUR RELATIONSHIP WITH YOUR SEXUALITY?

SACRAL

DAY 99

YOU GIVE YOURSELF PERMISSION TO FULLY ENJOY EVERYTHING THAT YOU DO

SACRAL

YOU ENJOY THE ABUNDANCE OF LIFE

SACRAL

DAY 101

IT IS SAFE FOR YOU TO FEEL ALL OF YOUR FEELINGS

SACRAL

DAY 102

YOU LOVE FLOWING MOVEMENTS THAT TAP YOU BACK INTO YOUR BODY

SACRAL

DAY 103

YOU ENJOY THE ABUNDANCE OF LIFE

SACRAL

YOU EMBRACE AND CELEBRATE YOUR SEXUALITY

SOLAR PLEXUS

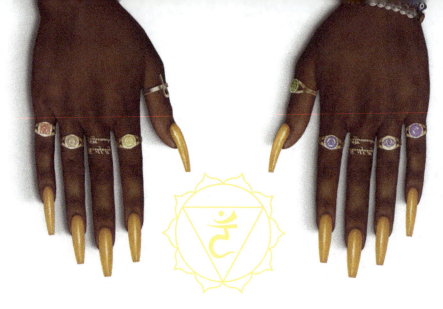

SOLAR PLEXUS

THE SUN INSIDE ME SHINES LIKE THE SUNLIGHT AT NOON

THE SUN INSIDE ME REMINDS ME THAT I AM DIVINE

THE SUN INSIDE ME MAKES CONFIDENCE GLOW LIKE GOLDEN RAYS

THE SUN INSIDE ME IS THE VITAMIN OF MY PERSONAL POWER

MORE CHAKRA INFORMATION AND REFLECTION PAGES AVAILABLE IN YOUR FAITHFULLY AFFIRMED JOURNAL

SOLAR PLEXUS

DAY 105

YOU ARE FREE FROM THE LIMITATIONS OF OTHERS

SOLAR PLEXUS

DAY 106

YOU OWN YOUR POWER AND RECOGNIZE THE STRENGTH AND BEAUTY IN WHO YOU ARE

SOLAR PLEXUS

DAY 107

YOU ARE A POWERFUL SOURCE OF LOVE AND LIGHT

SOLAR PLEXUS

DAY 108

YOU LOVE AND ACCEPT YOURSELF UNCONDITIONALLY

SOLAR PLEXUS

DAY 109

YOU ARE PROUD OF YOUR ACHEIVEMENTS

SOLAR PLEXUS

DAY 110

YOU ARE FREE TO CHOOSE

SOLAR PLEXUS

DAY 111

DIVINE POWER FLOWS THROUGH YOU

SOLAR PLEXUS

DAY 112

WHAT ARE 3 WAYS YOU CAN STRENGTHEN YOUR SELF-WORTH?

SOLAR PLEXUS

DAY 113

YOU RELEASE LIMITING BELIEFS AND REPLACE THEM WITH GRACE AND COMPASSION

SOLAR PLEXUS

DAY 114

YOUR BODY IS STRONG AND POWERFUL

SOLAR PLEXUS

DAY 115

YOU ENDURE IN TRIUMPH AGAINST ANY ADVERSITY

SOLAR PLEXUS

DAY 116

YOU CONFIDENTLY STAND IN YOUR OWN POWER

SOLAR PLEXUS

YOU ARE DIVINE POWER

SOLAR PLEXUS

DAY 118

YOU ARE SELF-AWARE WITH A STRONG SENSE OF SELF.

SOLAR PLEXUS

WHEN DO YOU FEEL THE MOST CONFIDENT?

SOLAR PLEXUS

DAY 120

YOU ACCEPT YOURSELF FOR WHO YOU ARE IN THIS MOMENT

SOLAR PLEXUS

DAY 121

YOU STEP INTO YOUR POWER CONFIDENTLY

SEE THE BEAUTY IN BEING YOU.

SOLAR PLEXUS

DAY 122

YOU CONFIDENTLY SHARE YOUR TALENTS AND GIFTS

SOLAR PLEXUS

DAY 123

YOU ARE A WELL-LOVED AND RESPECTED PERSON

SOLAR PLEXUS

DAY 124

YOUR DIGESTIVE SYSTEM IS STRONG AND HEALTHY

SOLAR PLEXUS

YOU HONOR AND SHARE YOUR UNIQUE GIFTS WITH THE WORLD

SOLAR PLEXUS

DAY 126

WHAT DOES SELF-RESPECT LOOK LIKE TO YOU? HOW DO YOU SHOW YOURSELF THAT DAILY?

SOLAR PLEXUS

DAY 127

YOU ARE SELF-AWARE WITH A STRONG SENSE OF SELF

SOLAR PLEXUS

DAY 128

YOU ARE THE EMBODIMENT OF PEACE AND CONFIDENCE

SOLAR PLEXUS

DAY 129

YOU MAINTAIN A HEALTHY GUT

SOLAR PLEXUS

DAY 130

YOU CAN CONNECT EASILY WITH THE SUN AND RADIANT LIGHT

SOLAR PLEXUS

DAY 131

YOU ARE MOTIVATED TO FULFILL YOUR PURPOSE

SEE THE BEAUTY IN BEING YOU

SOLAR PLEXUS

DAY 132

SEE THE BEAUTY IN BEING YOU.

YOU ARE WORTHY JUST AS YOU ARE

SOLAR PLEXUS

DAY 133

YOU ARE SUPPORTED IN ALL YOU DO IN LIFE

SOLAR PLEXUS

DAY 134

WHAT DOES IT MEAN TO BE A CONFIDENT PERSON?

SOLAR PLEXUS

DAY 135

YOUR LIFE PURPOSE IS DEMONSTRATED IN EVERYTHING THAT YOU DO

SOLAR PLEXUS

DAY 136

YOU TAKE PURPOSEFUL ACTION WITH EASE

SOLAR PLEXUS

DAY 137

YOU ARE COMFORTABLE IN YOUR POWER

SOLAR PLEXUS

DAY 138

YOU ARE AWARE OF YOUR OWN MIND

SOLAR PLEXUS

DAY 139

YOU APPROVE OF YOURSELF

SOLAR PLEXUS

DAY 140

YOUR SKIN EXUDES THE GLOW OF HEALTH

SOLAR PLEXUS

WHAT DOES IT MEAN TO BE IN YOUR PERSONAL POWER?

SOLAR PLEXUS

DAY 142

YOU MAINTAIN HIGH SELF ESTEEM BECAUSE YOU KNOW YOU ARE POWERFUL

SOLAR PLEXUS

DAY 143

YOU ALWAYS SHOW UP AS YOUR AUTHENTIC SELF

SOLAR PLEXUS

DAY 144

YOU ARE WORTHY OF THE COMPLIMENTS YOU RECEIVE

SOLAR PLEXUS

DAY 145

YOU EXPRESS YOURSELF IN A POWERFUL WAY

SOLAR PLEXUS

DAY 146

YOU CHOOSE TO ENJOY YOUR LIFE

SOLAR PLEXUS

DAY 147

YOU HAVE A CLEAR VISION

SOLAR PLEXUS

DAY 148

WHAT IS THE IMPORTANCE OF AUTONOMY?

SOLAR PLEXUS

DAY 149

YOU MAKE YOU OWN DECISIONS WITH CONVICTION AND CONFIDENCE

SOLAR PLEXUS

DAY 150

YOU ARE ENOUGH JUST AS YOU ARE AND YOU REMIND YOURSELF OF THAT WITH CONFIDENCE DAILY

SOLAR PLEXUS

YOU ARE A HAPPY AND SUCCESSFUL PERSON

SOLAR PLEXUS

DAY 152

YOU ARE KIND TO YOURSELF AND YOUR DEVELOPMENT

SOLAR PLEXUS

DAY 153

YOU STAND FIRM EVEN WHEN YOU ARE STANDING ALONE

SEE THE BEAUTY IN BEING YOU

SOLAR PLEXUS

DAY 154

YOU DO NOT NEED VALIDATION FROM OTHERS TO KNOW HOW GREAT AND WORTHY YOU ARE

SOLAR PLEXUS

DAY 155

IN WHAT AREAS OF LIFE CAN YOU IMPROVE YOUR SELF EMPOWERMENT? WRITE 3 WAYS TO HELP IMPLEMENT THAT CHANGE?

SOLAR PLEXUS

DAY 156

YOU WELCOME NEW EXPERIENCES WITH CONFIDENCE

SOLAR PLEXUS

DAY 157

YOU ARE A SACRED BEING

SOLAR PLEXUS

DAY 158

YOU FOLLOW YOUR OWN PATH TO SUCCESS AND FULFILLMENT

SOLAR PLEXUS

DAY 159

YOU ARE SOLUTION ORIENTED SO WHEN ISSUES ARISE YOU ARE ABLE TO SOLVE THEM

HEART CHAKRA

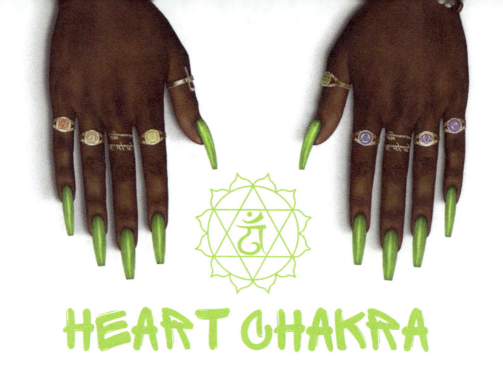

HEART CHAKRA

BEATING TO THE RHYTHM OF HEALING

PROVIDING AN OPEN SPACE FOR GRACE AND CURRENTS OF COMPASSION TO FILL MY CUP

DROWNING OUT PAST HURTS AND ALLOWING A LOVE THAT HAS ALWAYS EXISTED TO SURFACE

MORE CHAKRA INFORMATION AND REFLECTION PAGES AVAILABLE IN YOUR FAITHFULLY AFFIRMED JOURNAL

HEART

DAY 160

LOVE MOVES THROUGH YOU AND CONNECTS YOU TO THE SOURCE OF LIFE

HEART

DAY 161

YOU ALLOW LOVE TO COME INTO YOUR LIFE AND FILL YOU WITH HAPPINESS AND JOY

HEART

DAY 162

WHAT DOES IT MEAN TO YOU TO PUT YOUR FEELINGS AND NEEDS FIRST?

HEART

YOU ARE A MANIFESTATION OF PURE LOVE

HEART

DAY 164

YOU ARE LOVE

HEART

DAY 165

THE FEELING OF LOVE IS GROWING INSIDE OF YOU BECAUSE YOU ARE LOVE

HEART

IT IS SAFE TO LISTEN TO YOURSELF

HEART

DAY 167

YOU SMILE AT YOURSELF EVERYTIME YOU LOOK IN THE MIRROR

HEART

DAY 168

YOUR EMOTIONS GUIDE YOU TOWARDS HEALING FOR YOUR ENTIRE BEING

HEART

DAY 169

WHAT 5 MINUTE SELF CARE PRACTICE CAN YOU DO DAILY TO CULTIVATE FEELINGS OF UNCONDITIONAL LOVE?

HEART

DAY 170

IN EVERY DECISION YOU MAKE YOU ACCOUNT FOR YOURSELF FIRST

HEART

YOUR ESSENCE IS LOVE

HEART

DAY 172

YOU TOUCH YOUR HEART WITH LOVE AND COMPASSION TO ACKNOWLEDGE IT'S PRESENCE

SEE THE BEAUTY IN BEING YOU

HEART

DAY 173

YOU LOVE EVERY PART OF YOUR BEING

HEART

DAY 174

LOVE IS YOUR TRUE NATURE

HEART

YOU ARE AT PEACE

HEART

DAY 176

WHAT FEARS AND/OR LIMITING BELIEFS ARE KEEPING YOU FROM ACCEPTING UNCONDITIONAL LOVE?

HEART

DAY 177

YOU ARE HEALED BECAUSE YOU ARE LOVED

HEART

YOUR FUTURE IS BRIGHT

HEART

DAY 179

YOU TRUST IN LOVE

HEART

DAY 180

YOU ALLOW YOUR HEART CHAKRA TO LEAD YOU TO LOVE

HEART

DAY 181

YOU TREAT YOURSELF WITH CARE DAILY IN THE BEST WAY POSSIBLE

HEART

YOU DEEPLY AND COMPLETELY LOVE AND ACCEPT YOURSELF

HEART

DAY 183

HOW CAN YOU CULTIVATE THE FEELINGS OF PEACE IN YOUR EVERYDAY LIFE?

HEART

DAY 184

YOU PUT YOURSELF FIRST BECAUSE ONLY THEN CAN YOU GIVE TO OTHERS

HEART

THE LOVE YOU FEEL WITHIN IS DEEPER THAN ANYTHING YOU HAVE PERCEIVED OUTSIDE OF YOURSELF

HEART

DAY 186

YOU KNOW THAT TRUE LOVE IS THE LOVE YOU HAVE FOR YOURSELF

HEART

DAY 187

YOU ARE A LOVING AND MAGICAL BEING

HEART

YOU ALLOW YOUR HEART TO SPREAD THE FEELING OF LOVE THROUGHOUT YOUR ENTIRE BEING

HEART

YOUR PRESENCE IS LOVE

HEART

DAY 190

WHAT WERE YOU TAUGHT ABOUT GIVING AND RECEIVING LOVE AS A CHILD?

HEART

YOUR LOVING BODY SUPPORTS YOU THROUGHOUT YOUR LIFE. YOU ARE PROUD OF YOUR BODY

HEART

DAY 192

NO ONE ELSE CAN DICTATE HOW YOU LOVE YOURSELF

HEART

DAY 193

YOU LOVE YOURSELF FIRST WHICH ALLOWS YOU TO LOVE OTHERS

HEART

YOUR HEART INVITES YOU TO OPEN UP

HEART

YOU LOVE THE PERSON YOU ARE TODAY

HEART

DAY 196

YOU SHOW RESPECT TO YOUR HEART BY BEING PRESENT

HEART

DAY 197

WHAT IS YOUR BIGGEST FLAW IN RELATIONSHIPS WITH OTHERS?

HEART

THE LOVE THAT YOU NEED YOUR HEART CAN PROVIDE FOR YOU

HEART

DAY 199

YOUR HEART NEVER ASKS YOU TO SURRENDER TO LOVE OUTSIDE OF YOURSELF

HEART

THE LOVE THAT YOU FEEL FOR YOURSELF IS UNCONDITIONAL

HEART

YOU LOVE HOW LOVING AND COMPASSIONATE YOU ARE

HEART

EVERY CELL IN YOUR BODY VIBRATES WITH LOVE

HEART

DAY 203

YOU ALLOW YOUR HEART TO RELEASE PAST HURT

HEART

DO YOU FEEL WORTHY OF TRUE LOVE? WHY OR WHY NOT?

HEART

YOU EXPAND LOVE

HEART

DAY 206

YOUR HEART CHAKRA IS EXPANDING TOWARDS LOVE

HEART

YOU LISTEN TO YOUR HEART WITH EASE

HEART

YOU HAVE A BEAUTIFUL HEART

HEART

DAY 209

ANYTIME YOU DECIDE YOU CAN RETURN TO LOVE

HEART

YOU SURRENDER TO THE LOVE THAT YOU ARE

HEART

DAY 211

HOW DO YOU KNOW WHEN YOU ARE BEING LOVED PROPERLY?

HEART

BEING LEAD BY LOVE IS SAFE FOR YOU

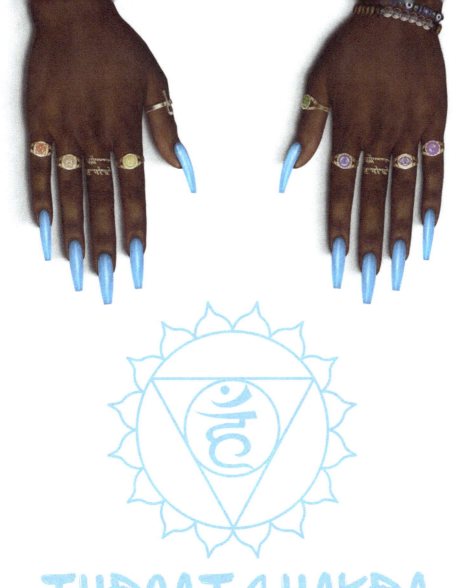

THROAT

COMMUNICATING MY TRUTH WITH DIVINE INTENTION
WHEN MY INNER VOICE SPEAKS MY SOUL LISTENS
RESCUING ME FROM THE DEPTHS OF SILENCE TRANSMUTING THE WHISPERS INTO FULL BLOWN POWER

MORE CHAKRA INFORMATION
AND REFLECTION PAGES
AVAILABLE IN YOUR
FAITHFULLY AFFIRMED
JOURNAL

THROAT

DAY 213

YOU RECLAIM YOUR VOICE AS YOUR OWN

THROAT

YOU RADIANT A BRIGHT BLUE ENERGY

THROAT

YOU SPEAK FREELY

THROAT

DAY 216

SPEAKING YOUR TRUTH SETS YOU FREE

THROAT

YOU COMMUNICATE ALL THAT YOU ARE

THROAT

IS THERE SOMETHING THAT YOU WANT TO EXPRESS TO SOMEONE BUT HAVE NEVER FOUND THE WORDS TO?
BE HONEST AND WRITE ABOUT WHAT'S HOLDING YOU BACK.

THROAT

YOU REJECT ANY PRESSURE TO BE SILENT

THROAT

DAY 220

AS YOU SPEAK UP DOORS OPEN FOR YOU

THROAT

YOU EMBODY TRUTH

THROAT

YOU RESPECT YOUR TRUTH

THROAT

YOU FIND IT EASIER TO EXPRESS YOUR THOUGHTS AND FEELINGS THE MORE YOU HONOR THEM

THROAT

DAY 224

YOU ARE NOT A PRISIONER OF OTHER PEOPLE'S WORDS

THROAT

DAY 225

IN WHAT SITUATIONS DO YOU HOLD BACK FROM SPEAKING YOUR TRUTH? HOW CAN YOU OVERCOME THAT?

THROAT

DAY 226

WHEN I AM LOOKING FOR THE WORDS TO SAY, I TUNE INTO MY THROAT CHAKRA SO THEY FLOW EASILY

THROAT

YOUR VOICE IS CLEAR AND STRONG

THROAT

YOU ARE COMFORTABLE WITH SILENCE

THROAT

YOUR THROAT CHAKRA IS CLEAR OF CONSTRAINTS

THROAT

YOU BREATHE EASILY AND EFFORTLESSLY

THROAT

YOU SPEAK IN A LOVING WAY TO YOURSELF AND THOSE AROUND YOU.

THROAT

DAY 232

HOW CAN YOU CULTIVATE MORE CONFIDENCE IN SITUATIONS WHERE YOU ARE CALLED TO SPEAK YOUR TRUTH?

THROAT

YOU ARE IN TOUCH WITH YOUR WANTS AND NEEDS AND SPEAK THEM IN A BOLD AND HEALTHY MANNER

THROAT

AS YOU SPEAK YOU STEP OUT OF FEAR INTO LIGHT

THROAT

DAY 235

YOU ARE AT EASE WHEN YOU SPEAK

THROAT

DAY 236

YOU SPEAK YOUR TRUTH WITH CONFIDENCE

THROAT

YOU ARE FREE TO SPEAK, THINK AND BE COMPLETELY YOU

THROAT

DAY 238

YOU ARE FULLY AWARE WHEN OTHERS SHARE THEIR TRUTH WITH YOU

THROAT

DAY 239

WHEN HAVE YOU SPOKE YOUR TRUTH AND FELT HEARD, RESPECTED AND LISTENED TO? HOW DID YOU FEEL?

THROAT

YOU COMMUNICATE WITH A OPEN HEART

THROAT

WHEN YOU SPEAK YOU PROJECT POWER

THROAT

DAY 242

YOU MAINTAIN INTEGRITY WHEN YOU SPEAK

THROAT

WHEN YOU SPEAK YOU MOVE INTO A STATE OF FLOW

THROAT

AS YOU TAKE OWNERSHIP OF YOUR VOICE YOU TAKE CONTROL OF YOUR LIFE

THROAT

DAY 245

YOUR VOICE, WORDS, IDEAS, AND PRESENCE MATTERS

THROAT

DAY 246

YOU SPEAK UP FOR YOURSELF AND WHAT YOU BELIEVE IN

THROAT

DAY 247

WHAT IS THE BIGGEST LIE YOU EVER TOLD AND WHY?

THROAT

DAY 248

YOU DESERVE TO SPEAK WHAT YOU FEEL AND WHAT YOU BELIEVE

THROAT

YOU HONOR YOUR VOICE AND NOURISH IT DAILY

THROAT

YOU ARE STRONG IN YOUR TRUTH

THROAT

DAY 251

AS YOU SPEAK YOUR VOICE RINGS LOUD AND CLEAR

THROAT

YOUR TRUTH RESONATES WITH THE UNIVERSE'S TRUTH

THROAT

DAY 253

YOUR VOICE BELONGS TO YOU

THROAT

YOUR THOUGHTS AND IDEAS ARE VALUABLE AND WORTHY OF EXPRESSION

THROAT

DAY 255

HOW DOES THE FOLLOWING STATEMENT MAKE YOU FEEL?

'YOU DESERVE TO SPEAK UP AND BE LISTENED TO.'

WHY DO YOU FEEL THIS WAY?

THROAT

DAY 256

YOUR VOICE DESERVES TO BE HEARD

THROAT

YOU ENJOY EXPRESSING WHO YOU ARE

THROAT

YOUR VOICE IS RELAXED AND CALM WHEN NECCESSARY

THROAT

DAY 259

WORDS FLOW TO YOU EASILY

THROAT

YOU ACKNOWLEDGE THE POWER OF YOUR WORDS AND USE YOUR POWER WISELY

THROAT

DAY 261

YOUR THROAT CHAKRA IS AS OPEN AS THE BLUE SKY ON A CLEAR SUNNY DAY

THROAT

DAY 262

WHAT DOES IT MEAN TO BE AUTHENTIC?

THROAT

DAY 263

YOU EXPRESS YOURSELF OPENLY

THROAT

DAY 264

IN BOTH SPEECH AND SILENCE YOU RADIATE TRUTH

THROAT

DAY 265

SPEAKING YOUR TRUTH HAS BECOME A NATURAL ACT OF BEING

THROAT

DAY 266

YOU DO NOT ALLOW SOMEONE ELSE'S TRUTH TO ALTER YOURS

THIRD EYE CHAKRA

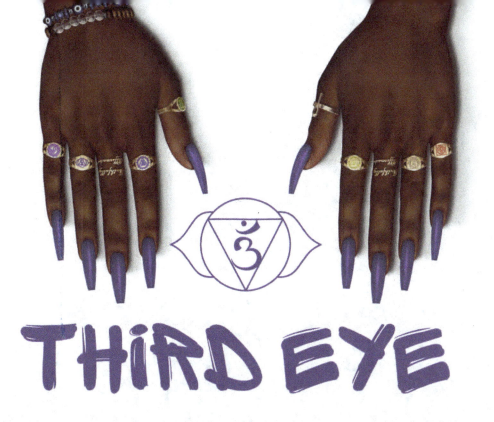

THIRD EYE

WISDOM DEEP ENOUGH TO GRACE AN OCEAN FLOOR
YET ELEVATED ENOUGH TO REACH MY HIGHEST CONSCIOUSNESS
REFLECTING THE ANSWERS OF THE UNSEEN
IN A VOICE THAT ONLY MY SPIRIT CAN RECEIVE

MORE CHAKRA INFORMATION
AND REFLECTION PAGES
AVAILABLE IN YOUR
FAITHFULLY AFFIRMED
JOURNAL

3RD EYE
CHAKRA

YOUR SPIRITUAL ABILITIES ARE SAFE TO HAVE

3RD EYE CHAKRA

DAY 268

THE ANSWERS YOU SEEK ARE ALWAYS WITHIN YOU

3RD EYE
CHAKRA

YOU NURTURE YOUR SPIRIT AND ARE IN TUNE WITH ITS NEEDS

3RD EYE
CHAKRA

DAY 270

WHEN YOU ARE LOOKING FOR ANSWERS YOU TAP INTO YOUR INNER WISDOM

3RD EYE CHAKRA

YOUR MIND IS STRONG, OPEN, AND CLEAR

3RD EYE
CHAKRA

DAY 272

YOU HAVE INFINITE WISDOM

3RD EYE
CHAKRA

YOU MOVE IN YOUR LIFE WITH GRACE AND EASE

3RD EYE
CHAKRA

DAY 274

YOU VIEW YOUR OBSTACLES AS OPPORTUNITIES TO GET CLOSER TO GOD

3RD EYE CHAKRA

DAY 275

YOU ARE COMFORTABLE MAKING DECISIONS

3RD EYE
CHAKRA

DAY 276

VISUALIZE YOUR PERFECT LIFE. WHAT DOES IT LOOK LIKE?

3RD EYE CHAKRA

DAY 277

YOU RECEIVE GUIDANCE AND PROTECTION AT ALL TIMES

3RD EYE
CHAKRA

DAY 278

YOU RELEASE THE MENTAL CLUTTER THAT PREVENTS YOU FROM TAPPING INTO YOUR INNER WISDOM

3RD EYE
CHAKRA

YOU ALLOW YOURSELF TO ONLY SEE THE TRUTH

3RD EYE
CHAKRA

DAY 280

YOUR THIRD EYE SEES ALL

3RD EYE
CHAKRA

DAY 281

YOU QUIET YOUR MIND WITH EASE

3RD EYE CHAKRA

DAY 282

YOU TRUST THE INSIGHT YOU GET FROM YOUR INTUITION

3RD EYE CHAKRA

HOW IS YOUR RELATIONSHIP WITH YOUR INTUITION?

3RD EYE
CHAKRA

DAY 284

YOU ARE DECISIVE

3RD EYE
CHAKRA

YOU HAVE A HEALTHY RELATIONSHIP WITH YOUR INNER COMPASS

3RD EYE
CHAKRA

DAY 286

YOU ARE IN ALIGNMENT WITH YOUR PURPOSE

3RD EYE
CHAKRA

DAY 287

YOU ACCEPT YOURSELF EXACTLY AS YOU ARE

3RD EYE
CHAKRA

DAY 288

ALL THAT YOU SEEK YOU CAN FIND WITHIN YOURSELF

3RD EYE
CHAKRA

DAY 289

YOU HONOR YOUR INTUITION AND USE IT AS A GUIDE

3RD EYE
CHAKRA

DAY 290

WOULD YOU LIKE TO BE MORE INTUITIVE? WHY OR WHY NOT?

3RD EYE
CHAKRA

DAY 291

YOU ARE WISE

3RD EYE
CHAKRA

DAY 292

YOU ALLOW YOURSELF TO SEE THE TRUTH

3RD EYE
CHAKRA

DAY 293

CLARITY IS YOUR BIRTH RIGHT

3RD EYE CHAKRA

DAY 294

YOU LISTEN TO YOUR INNER KNOWING IN THE FACE OF UNCERTAINTY

3RD EYE
CHAKRA

DAY 295

YOU SEE YOURSELF AS YOU ARE

3RD EYE
CHAKRA

DAY 296

IT IS SAFE FOR YOU TO SEE

3RD EYE
CHAKRA

IN WHAT WAYS DOES FEAR TRY TO PROTECT YOU? HOW CAN YOU TELL WHEN YOU SHOULD LISTEN TO THAT?

3RD EYE CHAKRA

DAY 298

YOU ACT IN ACCORDANCE WITH YOUR INSPIRATION AND DIVINE PURPOSE

3RD EYE CHAKRA

DAY 299

YOU EASILY VISUALIZE YOUR DESIRES

3RD EYE
CHAKRA

DAY 300

YOU HAVE DISCERNMENT

3RD EYE
CHAKRA

DAY 301

YOU ARE PROPHETIC

3RD EYE CHAKRA

DAY 302

YOUR INTUITIVE SENSES ARE AWAKENED

3RD EYE CHAKRA

DAY 303

YOU RECOGNIZE MULTIPLE PERSPECTIVES IN EVERY SITUATION

3RD EYE
CHAKRA

DAY 304

DO YOU TRUST YOURSELF TO MAKE GOOD DECISIONS? WHY OR WHY NOT?

3RD EYE
CHAKRA

YOU SURRENDER TO THE DIVINE

3RD EYE
CHAKRA

DAY 306

YOU ARE OPTIMISTIC AND UNAFRAID OF THE UNKNOWN

3RD EYE
CHAKRA

DAY 307

YOU LISTEN TO YOUR INNER VOICE AND ALLOW IT TO GUIDE YOU TO PURPOSE, PEACE, AND HAPPINESS

3RD EYE CHAKRA

DAY 308

YOUR THIRD EYE SEES ALL

IT NEEDS TO SEE

WHEN IT NEEDS TO SEE IT

3RD EYE
CHAKRA

DAY 309

YOU HAVE A CLEAR MIND

3RD EYE
CHAKRA

DAY 310

YOU ACKNOWLEDGE YOUR PLACE IN THE WORLD WITH PLEASURE

3RD EYE CHAKRA

IN WHAT WAYS DO YOU MISTRUST YOUR INTUITION?

3RD EYE
CHAKRA

DAY 312

YOU ARE OPEN TO YOUR HIGHEST AWARENESS AND LISTEN

3RD EYE
CHAKRA

DAY 313

YOUR INNER WISDOM GUIDES YOU TO YOUR HIGHEST GOOD

3RD EYE
CHAKRA

DAY 314

YOU ARE LIVING IN HARMONY WITH YOURSELF

3RD EYE
CHAKRA

DAY 315

YOU ARE THE SOURCE OF YOUR TRUTH AND YOUR LOVE

3RD EYE CHAKRA

DAY 316

YOU ARE ABLE TO SEE AND ACT IN ALIGNMENT WITH YOUR DIVINE PURPOSE

3RD EYE
CHAKRA

DAY 317

YOU ARE AN EXTENSION OF GOD WHO CHOOSES TO ACCEPT GOD'S KINDNESS AND LOVE

3RD EYE CHAKRA

DAY 318

YOU ALLOW OTHERS TO BE IN THEIR TRUTH

3RD EYE CHAKRA

DAY 319

HOW COULD YOU IMPROVE YOUR RELATIONSHIP WITH YOUR INTUITION?

CROWN

I HAVE THE RIGHT TO BASK IN MY OWN
ENERGY AND EMBRACE MY FULLEST
EXPRESSION
THROUGH THIS CONNECTION COMES
ASCENSION
LEAVING ME OPEN TO DIVINE ALIGNMENT
AND WISDOM

MORE CHAKRA INFORMATION
AND REFLECTION PAGES
AVAILABLE IN YOUR
FAITHFULLY AFFIRMED
JOURNAL

CROWN

DAY 320

YOU CONSCIOUSLY CREATE YOUR LIFE WITH LOVE

CROWN

DAY 321

YOU EXPERIENCE EVERYTHING WITH GRACE

CROWN

INFORMATION COMES TO YOU EASILY

CROWN

DAY 323

YOU SEEK TO UNDERSTAND AND LEARN FROM YOUR EXPERIENCES

CROWN

YOU ARE YOUR HIGHEST AND MOST AUTHENTIC SELF

CROWN

YOU ARE JOY

CROWN

HOW DO YOU COMMUNICATE WITH THE UNIVERSE?

CROWN

DAY 327

YOU ARE AT PEACE

CROWN

DAY 328

YOU ARE MORE THAN YOUR EGO

CROWN

DAY 329

YOU ARE LOVE

CROWN

DAY 330

YOU ARE INFINITE

CROWN

DAY 331

YOU ARE GRATEFUL FOR THE ABUNDANCE THAT SURROUNDS YOU

CROWN

DAY 332

YOU UNDERSTAND AND OVERSTAND YOUR DEEPER TRUTH AND CONNECTION

CROWN

DAY 333

HOW DOES THE UNIVERSE COMMUNICATE WITH YOU?

CROWN

DAY 334

YOU ARE A MAGNIFICENT CREATION OF THE UNIVERSE

CROWN

DAY 335

YOU ARE AT PEACE, WHOLE, AND BALANCED

CROWN

DAY 336

YOU ARE GUIDED BY YOUR INNER WISDOM

CROWN

DAY 337

YOU ARE A CELESTIAL BEING WITH INFINITE POTENTIAL

CROWN

DAY 338

YOU ARE LIGHT

CROWN

DAY 339

YOU LIVE IN THE PRESENT MOMENT

CROWN

DESCRIBE YOUR HIGHEST SELF?

CROWN

DAY 341

ETERNAL PEACE FLOWS TO AND THROUGH YOU

CROWN

YOU HONOR THE SACRED LIGHT WITHIN YOU AND ALL BEINGS

CROWN

DAY 343

YOU ARE WHOLE AND ONE WITH DIVINE ENERGY

CROWN

DAY 344

YOU ARE ONE WITH ALL OF LIFE

CROWN

DAY 345

YOU EMBRACE YOUR SPIRITUAL SELF AND EARTHLY SELF

CROWN

DAY 346

YOU SEEK EXPERIENCES THAT NOURISH YOUR SPIRIT

CROWN

HOW DOES YOUR HIGHEST SELF SHOW UP IN THE WORLD?

CROWN

DAY 348

YOU ARE CONNECTED TO A LIMITLESS SOURCE OF CREATIVITY, ABUNDANCE, HEALTH, HAPPINESS, AND LOVE

CROWN

DAY 349

YOU ALLOW GOOD TO UNFOLD IN YOUR LIFE BY EXPRESSING GRATITUDE

CROWN

DAY 350

YOU ARE COMPLETE AND ONE WITH DIVINE ENERGY

CROWN

DAY 351

YOU ARE PROTECTED AND GUIDED AT ALL TIMES

CROWN

DAY 352

YOU ARE EXPANDING WITH THE UNIVERSE

CROWN

DAY 353

YOU HAVE SIGNIFICANCE IN THE WORLD

CROWN

DAY 354

DO YOU COMMUNICATE WITH YOUR HIGHEST SELF ABOUT YOUR ACTIONS AND DECISIONS? WHY OR WHY NOT?

CROWN

DAY 355

YOU ARE ALIGNED WITH YOUR SOUL'S PURPOSE AND TRUTH

CROWN

YOU HONOR THE SACRED DIVINITY WITHIN YOU

CROWN

DAY 357

YOU ARE WORTHY BECAUSE YOU EXIST

CROWN

DAY 358

YOU SURRENDER THE HOW AND WHEN OF MANIFESTATIONS TO THE UNIVERSE

CROWN

DAY 359

YOU ARE OPEN TO DIVINE KNOWLEDGE, INSIGHTS, VISIONS, AND WISDOM

CROWN

DAY 360

YOU ARE A SPIRITUAL BEING IN A HUMAN BODY THAT HONORS THE HUMAN EXPERIENCE

CROWN

DAY 361

WHAT DOES 'SURRENDERING', LOOK LIKE FOR YOU?

CROWN

YOU UNDERSTAND AND OVERSTAND THAT WE ARE ALL CONNECTED

CROWN

DAY 363

YOU ARE RAISING YOUR LEVEL OF CONSCIOUSNESS DAILY

CROWN

DAY 364

YOU ARE OPEN TO LETTING GO OF ATTACHMENTS

CROWN

DAY 365

YOU INVITE AND ALLOW DIVINE ENERGY TO BE AROUND YOU AND FLOW THROUGH YOU

CROWN

DAY 366

HOW MIGHT YOU BE BLOCKING GRACE?

ACKNOWLEDGMENTS

SOMEWHERE BETWEEN 2018 AND 2020 THIS BOOK WAS PLANTED INSIDE OF ME. AS SOMEONE WHO SPENDS A LOT OF TIME ALONE, THERE WERE TONS OF MOMENTS I CRAVED AFFIRMATIONS FROM SOMEONE BESIDES THE PERSON IN THE MIRROR. NOT THAT SHE WASN'T ENOUGH. IT'S JUST THAT HER SIGHT GOT A BIT DISTORTED.

I THOUGHT THIS WOULD BE SOMETHING I STARTED ON YOUTUBE YEARS AGO. BUT THE BLUR GOT THICKER AND THIS BOOK DID NOT YET EXIST. I AM PROUD TO TELL THAT QUEEN IN THE MIRROR THAT WE DID IT. NOT JUST FOR US BUT ALSO FOR THOSE WHO HAS MOMENTS OF NEEDING TO BE REAFFIRMED AND REASSURED. GLAD THAT THE ATTEMPTS TO GIVE UP WERE UNSUCCESSFUL.

GOD, ONLY YOU AND I TRULY KNOW THE JOURNEY I HAVE BEEN ON. I WANT TO THANK YOU FOR KEEPING ME. THANK YOU FOR NOT TURNING YOUR BACK ON ME EVEN WHEN I TURNED MY BACK ON YOU BECAUSE I FELT LET DOWN BY YOU. THANK YOU FOR TRUSTING ME WITH SUCH A DIVINE PURPOSE. I AM HAPPY THAT I FIXED MY RELATIONSHIP WITH YOU AND OF COURSE YOU WERE WITH ME THE ENTIRE TIME FILLING ME WITH YOUR PATIENT AND UNCONDITIONAL LOVE.

A SPECIAL THANK YOU TO IGNITED INK 717 FOR HELPING ME BRING THIS PROJECT TO LIFE. I APPRECIATE YOU FOR DEALING WITH ME AND CHALLENGING ME TO OWN MY POTENTIAL.

TO MY FAMILY. THANK YOU FOR BEING IN MY CORNER AND SEEING ME EVEN WHEN I COULDN'T SEE ME. YOU WERE MY STRENGTH WHEN I COULDN'T BE IT FOR ME. YOUR EFFORTS DOES NOT GO UNNOTICED.

TO ANYONE WHO HAD A HAND IN MAKING THIS COME TO LIFE; THANK YOU!

THANK YOU FOR BUYING THIS BOOK. I HOPE IT BLESSED YOU!

ABOUT THE AUTHOUR

SKYY DANIELLE, BORN IN FORT WORTH, TX AND MOLDED IN HOUSTON, TX IS MANY THINGS. A HEALING ENTHUSIAST, ENTREPRENEUR, POET, AUTHOR, PODCASTER, SPEAKER, MENTOR, LOVER OF AFFIRMATIONS AND A STUDENT OF LIFE. ALTHOUGH THOSE TITLES ARE AMAZING, THE NUMBER ONE THING SHE WANTS PEOPLE TO EMBRACE IS THAT SHE'S A SPIRITUAL BEING HAVING A HUMAN EXPERIENCE. SHE USES HER VOICE AND SPIRITUAL ABILITIES GIVEN TO HER BY GOD TO REACH THOSE WHOM SHE IS MEANT TO COME INTO CONTACT WITH. HER BRAND FAITHFUL BEAUTY AT FACE VALUE SEEMS LIKE AN ACCESSORY LINE. HOWEVER, SKYY IS VERY MUCH A GIRLS GIRL SO WOMEN EMPOWERMENT AND SELF LOVE IS AT THE FOUNDATION OF IT. SHE CONTINUES TO BE VULNERABLE ABOUT HER JOURNEY SO THOSE WHO WILL GO THROUGH OR HAVE GONE THROUGH SIMILAR EXPERIENCES DO NOT FEEL ALONE. SOMETHING SHE KNOWS ALL TO WELL BASED ON HER EXPERIENCE BEING AN ONLY CHILD. EVEN IN THE DAYS SHE STRUGGLED TO EMPOWER HERSELF SHE DESIRED TO CREATE SOMETHING TO HELP OTHER WOMEN/YOUNG LADIES COPE IN A HEALTHY MANNER. SHE WILL CONTINUE TO PUSH HER MISSION OF REACHING WOMEN AND YOUNG LADIES IN THE PURSUIT OF IGNITING FIRES IN THEIR HEARTS THAT INSPIRES THEM TO BE AUTHENTICALLY AND UNAPOLOGETICALLY THEMSELVES.

P.S. YOU MAY HEAR HER SAY UNIVERSE, ETC QUITE A BIT HOWEVER, SHE IS SPEAKING OF GOD.

TAKE SOME TIME TO AFFIRM YOURSELF….WRITE SOME SELF AFFIRMING AFFIRMATIONS ON THE NEXT TWO PAGES!